The Collected Poems
of James T. Farrell

The Collected Poems of James T. Farrell

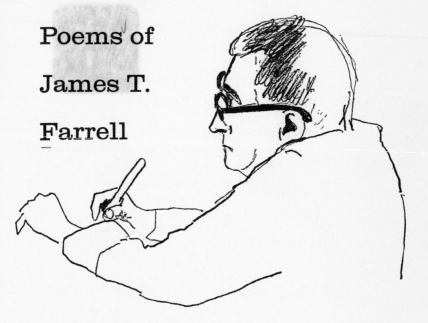

Fleet Publishing Corporation

NEW YORK

*The following publications have kindly granted permission
to reprint poems which originally appeared in their pages:
American Book Collector (Protest); Clyde Magazine (Bughouse
Square Chicago: 1930); English Journal (Happy Sunday, Wearied
World, Midnight—which appeared under the title, Form Of Love
And Life); Focus/Midwest (Night Mood, Night Scene, There Was
Only The Sunlight) © 1962 by Focus/Midwest Publishing
Company, Inc.; Genesis West (On A Possibly Trite Subject);
Phoenix (Stars Came Out At Night, Jackson Park—which
appeared under the title, Spring Poem); Raleigh News & Observer
(Moonlight Soliloquy, Lettre A François Villon); Statement
(Moonlight Soliloquy); The Carleton Miscellany (Golden Youth:
1794); The Critic (Gethsemane); The New York Herald Tribune
(Summer Morning: Wind); The New York Times (Night Mood,
Night Scene, There Was Only The Sunlight, Moonlight Soliloquy,
Winter Evening, Midnight—which appeared under the title, Form
Of Love And Life); Thought Magazine (Moonlight Soliloquy,
Words to Yorick's Brothers); United Press International
(My Obituary); Hawk and Whippoorwill (Is April
Only Anguish).*

This book is
dedicated to Neda Westlake and
Louise Richmond

CONTENTS

The Collected Poems
of James T. Farrell

Sights

I am one who sits and watches
I see many things; and I see nothing.
I see an old man who sits before a shuttle, spinning
　　black threads into a useless web.
I see little children laughing at this man.
I see a circus full of clowns, who never vary their
　　jokes—or their acts.
I see the loves of men and women bloom like roses
　　in June.
I see the loves of men and women wither like the
　　shrivelled roses of October.

I see dreams circling the sun.

I see dreams crashing to the earth with broken wings.

I see rainbows fading into a colorless mist.

I see purple vapored bubbles bursting.

I see men running away from a bottomless pit.

I see an endless confusion.

I see these pictures as a mirror reflecting myself.

I see everything vanishing like smoke.

I see everything returning.

I see an endless recurrence of many things and of nothing.

1927

Protest

I sit at the window of a filling station and laugh
  with happiness.
A beautiful storm snarls on my corner,
I welcome this storm,
It sings for me a wild hymn of protest,
The protest is against my corner.
It is an ugly and hideous corner, with groaning
  street cars, vulgar signs and cold buildings.
It is like a young brute with iron shoulders, thick
  lips that only know curses and a dirty face.

It is a young brute:

But the storm slaps its face.

I laugh.

Witch-eyed clouds pelt the gloomy factory across
the street with rain,

I like that.

The building is a stone cage, that shuts out the
sunlight and withers young girls.

The viking wind shakes the advertising signs until
they shiver.

I like that, too.

These signs are part of the lie-structure called
progress.

The rain is a whip.

The thunder is a wild oath.

The lightning is a snake eye.

With these, the storm chases people into doorways.

The faces of people are sad: and sadden me.

The storm is a bellowing, clamoring, roaring,
raving, snarling, bruising, battering, screeching,
shouting, snorting monster.

It slaps the dirty face of my ugly corner.

1927

In vitam aeternam

He sits at his desk, in his office,
Nearby to God's office in Heaven,
And he reads his press clippings.
Who is he, what's his name?
He is, his name is
Studs Lonigan.

1964

Happy Sunday

Like a woman, laughing and fulfilled,
The spring grows over the indolent Sunday street,
A string of gold about her hair,
A band of green around her feet.
She has drained into her womb
The secrets of winter's seeds,
And she comes, laughing and fulfilled.

1929

Sunday afternoon

There was an efficiency
To the sullen lake
That dragged its foam-topped waves
Up to a rocky beach.

There was a poetry
To the children flinging stones,
And greeting each plop and splash
With a sudden screech.

There was a misery
To the bulging man and wife.

Climbing jagged rocks—
Their faces cancelled speech.

There was, to me
An accident of atoms
Awaiting that shot
That blasts death's last breach.

1929

On a possibly trite subject

This rose I offer you—
Unimaginative symbol of a mood
Worn into an old, old groove—
Accept
And poise it in your swirl of hair
Where it is free of earthly dirt
That traps its thousand brothers,
For you and I
Like this rose, walk in the loam
Of nature's laws,

Yet we would poise love
In a golden swirl
Untrapped.

1929

Nostalgic mood

These slight spring winds
Form a frail and trembling bridge
To yesterday.
Across their precarious stretch
I move
Delicate sentiments
That shudder
With the swinging bridge
And their own shaking weakness.
Yet they move relentlessly—

At my command—
Back to you.

1929-30

There was only the sunlight

There was only the sunlight
Pressing through a dirty pane
And the spring day
Swirling over rumbling traffic
And myself
In a messy room
With coffee grounds
And cigarette butts
And scattered books
And we three

Sun
And Spring
And I
Formed a trinity of laughter.

1929-30

Winter evening

Girl
Before your window
Was the January street,
Piled with snow.
We sipped our coffee
And discussed the Swedish rye bread;
And forgot the dream
That death can slide into each head
To beat, and to beat.
And light and shadow made your head

15

One lovely
Swirl.
You spoke of love.
I thought of faith and hope.
We spoke,
We two, formed to grope
Within the limits of a circled January street
Where death is . . . oh, so sleek.

1929

Moonlight soliloquy

World, Earth, God!
I can view scraps of you
Through a dusty window;
Through time's dusty frame of my shifting days
To hopeful ways
Where faith is poised and kind.
World, beyond your scraps,
I watch the pretended kindness of a moon
That winds and clouds have shred
Into fragile tints of vapor.

17

And I name it the symbol
Of the only faith you grant
To those you fret and break.
Tonight there is rest
And a promise of more rest,
Amid those soundless grasses
That sleep beyond our parting paths.
World, the only final faith you offer
Is death that charms with its alien emptiness.

1929

Midnight

Bare, bare, stripped process
Seems this callow world;
And my tired body does not care.
My burning eyes close
From resting pictures of starlight
Painting heavy shadows.
My flesh shrinks from cool lake breezes;
And melody is noise.
The midnight seals our dusty room,
And only your hot whiteness
Is real.

1929

Picture

Moonlight
Rides the sky tonight
Lancing the sleep
Of this one, weak tree
With easy practiced strokes.

1929

Homecoming

Heads were bowed in the gloomy Sunday
   station:
Tears rolled down age-cancelled cheeks:
And prayers were muttered:
Cameras clicked:
And reporters scribbled down superlatives.
Live heroes fired a solemn salute;
And a blind veteran sounded taps.
While s-l-o-w-l-y,
S-o-l-e-m-n-l-y,

21

Five flag-draped boxes
Of rattling bones and odorous flesh
Were carted away.
No one remembered,
No one protested,
No one asked
Why they died;
Not even relatives still proud of their sadness.
Glory smothered the return
Of these dead heroes to "their final resting place."
Glory covered these Archangel casualties,
These murdered chumps of their country's folly,
Who came home today,
Earning with their forgotten lives,
One day's notice in the Chicago Herald Examiner.
They came home—
Five silent boxes of bones
Uttering . . .
                    Nothing.

1929-30

On the memorial services of
Harrison M. Weil, dead organist

Leave him be,
You spewing reverends,
Doddering on death's edge yourself.
Wound not the memory of this suicide failure,
Strew not false flowers of praise
On his casketed name.
Forget him
As he wished to be forgotten.
He is gone,
Gone by those hands

That vainly ached to do the bidding
Of Bach and Brahms and Palestrina.
He is gone, gone to oblivion,
Deep in forgetfulness of the heavy bodies
That trod this earth in brief nightmares.
He shed his failure like a man,
And departed hurt but brave.
Leave him be,
You cassocked noisemakers.
Forget him.

1929

Before babes became chicks

There she is
Primping,
Powdering,
Painting,
Singing,
In her seven-per-week hall room
That's all gloom.
And now she's leaving
To go dancing
At Guyon's Paradise,

She with a face for a magazine queen,
And a form for sculpture,
Dancing with strangers
At a public dance hall.
And next Saturday night
She will be
Primping,
Powdering,
Painting,
Singing,
To go dancing
And flaming—
A bird of Guyon's Paradise.

1929

Taxi dance saxophone

The jazz this saxophone vomits,
Is not happy.
It is a moan
And groan
And stabbing drone.
It is worn and tired madness
Seeking cheap, illusory gladness.
It is the call from tired, frazzled work
To crude sex dancing.
It soothes those

Who will sleep tonight with whores,
And hate themselves
When dawn
Slobbers
Through dirty windows
In cheap rooms
To point cold fingers at their disgust.
That is what this taxi-dance saxophone means
When it blares this devastation of noise.
It is a bray for those
Who plod the streets of cities
Reeking with murdered souls.

1929

Night scene

Slowly, a fog
Descends to clog
The April meaning of the night.
The corner light
Is splayed and feeble.
Buildings have shed the dignity of form
And hulk like enemies
Before the slow advance of quivering grayness.
People all walk, assuming
The mystery of shadows.

Down the quiet street, creeps
The disturbance of a motor car
With weakened yellow eyes,
And a whining engine, like a voice of Hell
Just above the formlessness of a hotel.
The mood rides softly
Through a cloud of tinted vapor.

1929-30

I vowed

I vowed that I would pave my solitude
With honesty and dignity;
And that I would love life
And laugh and dance
My spirit out in one gay rout.
I said that I would be gay and free
To rip the veils aside
And stare into a bare eternity.
Vows that cracked
Like frail glasses shattering

31

From the boiled water that they could not hold.
One by one, the years pile over me
Cancelling all that I have said,
Smothering me in that last, dark bed.

1929-30

Bughouse Square Chicago: 1930

If these men pray,
It is a prayer to slay
Memory.

If these men hope,
It is subtle dope
to deaden
Memory.

I walk the square,
And watch their faces,
Blankly contemplating
Empty spaces.

In every slumped and filthy body,
There is the tacit cry . . .
Let me forget.
Scattered on benches and grass,
They sit, and sleep, and stare, and talk, and wait
For time to take the sun away.
This guy calls the mayor a sonofabitch,
And that one says he's another.
Where's Hoover's prosperity? asks one.
His buddy points to the stinking lavatory:
In there, says he.
A pin-face works a cross-word puzzle;
And two punks argue about Lucky Strikes.
Three slavs preach revolution,
And a fourth gives them the razz.
A black buck sings jazz;
And an old man flops on the grass,
And looks at nowhere.
A peg-leg ogles a two-bit Susie.
An old hag scratches a tooth-pick leg,
And a grey beard watches her.
Two kids wonder whether they'll go
To New York or Frisco.

34

All day they wait,
And scrounge nickels for coffee and smokes,
And wait
            for night.
All night they sit, and stare, and talk, and maybe
    they sleep,
On newspaper pillows,
With newspaper blankets,
Their shoes stuffed with newspapers.

1930

The unremembering stars

Dreams,
I can dream them, too.
Dreams,
I can dream beyond the glory of the stars,
But dreams all shall die,
Before the stars shall die.
Dreams die hard in me.
There are no dreams in the unremembering stars.

1961

Night mood

Here spreads the lake,
Blue, calm, insensate.
Pile-driving stone shores
And receding, receding,
And there stands the night-lost survey of my city
With proud steelstone mounds
Framing a human petulance
That digs, pounds, shovels, builds
In sly escape from that whining why
That breaks our hearts on walls and laws of nerve-
  less matter.

Between the lake and city,
I move
Alone,
Homeless,
Caged,
Watching that far serenity
Of an untouched, ending world
Where lake and sky meet
Into false mysteries
Of freedom.

1930

Summer morning: wind

I hear the wind,
Singing the summer morning
Onward,
Forward,
Singing the summer morning,
And singing all and everything,
Singing all of the world,
Toward
And to

The Always Forever Silence of Silence.

The dying sun is warm and golden this morning.

1961

Is April only anguish

A gain,
Spring . . .
And we now are living in the nearest, closest
   April of our lives.
The days are clear.
The air is flooded with inundating sunlight.
But neither we nor April live forever.
And Oh! I know!
From all the dead April of our years
There are those unhealed, unhealing wounds

That bleed anguish
Only to bleed more anguish,
Because of the hopes that we merely hoped
Into hopelessness.
And because of the dreams that we only dreamed
Into emptiness.
And because of the loves that we loved
Into lovelessness.
But,
Again,
Spring . . .

We need not be dead
Until we die.

1962

Lettre à François Villon

C*hèr Maître Villon*
Vous avez dit
"Mais où sont les neiges d'antan?"
Melted,
Dear Villon,
They are melted
And since that day you swung,
The snows of many days,
And the snows of many years,
And the snows of centuries,

All, all are melted.
Mais alors:
François Villon
Homme condamné
Pauvre pendu
Poet éternal
Your pure clear songs
Are
Unmelted.

1962

My obituary

One James (T. for Thomas) Farrell
Who might have been this,
And who might have been that,
But who might have been
Neither this nor that,
And who wrote too much,
And who fought too much,
And who kissed too much,
For all of his friends,
(He needed no enemies)—

That man, J. T. F.
Died last night
Of a deprivation of time.
He willed his dust
To the public domain.

1962

Willie Collins speaking

Not one of them muckety mucks
Over at the main office
Who demoted me
And not one of them Route Inspectors
   and Wagon Dispatchers
The ones I didn't like
If you know what I mean
Not one mother's son of 'em
And Blubber-Guts, Bloated Belly, Gashouse
   McGinty,

Who tried to rub my nose in his horse turds
After I was demoted to drivin' a tractor,
Not one of 'em,
One mother's son of 'em
Smoked my cigars,
At my wake
On my insurance money.
While they was pushin' up daisies
With their toes straight up in the air,
I was pickin' my teeth
With my feet planted under the table,
In my own home
Where I was lord and master
If you know what I mean,
I outlived every one of 'em,
Every mother's son of 'em,
So who won in the end?
No flowers, please!
Willie Collins speaking.

1962

Stars came out at night

I cannot be the poet
That I might have been
When I was young,
When I knew the world
Must be sad with wonder.
But now,
I have lived the sad wonder of the world.
The stars came out at night
When I could have thought
That they trembled with a lustre

Only for you.
The stars came out at night
As they shall tonight.
And all of this resplendence
Is but the speed of light
And the hunger that is ours,
And that shifts from heart to eye.

1962

Sometimes

Sometimes
I like to count the names
Of all the dames
That I have laid
Away in my memory.
And I like to think of them
And love them all,
All over, once again,
In memory.
But what is it I do,

But dawdle and dabble
With the arithmetic
Of memory.
The ones I got,
Well, they were got,
And half-forgotten.
It's the ones I didn't get
Who give me my regret.

1962

Tendrement

Oh, *Genèvieve!*
Ma chère amie
Très chère amie;
Très, très gentille.
In Paris,
Please go, my dear,
A l'église de Sainte Genèvieve
And light a candle
Before Mary's altar,
And think

That I have lit it
For you,
Because we cannot say
What we would say
With words,
In any language,
We cannot say a flame,
We cannot speak a burning flame,
Gold, and red, and burning white—
Unspoken feelings
Unspoken loves;
Oh, Genèvieve!
Oh, Seigneur!

1963

Words to Yorick's brothers

It is easy to lose
And to live a social lie
In the defeated bitterness
Of money.
And it is safe
To crack your soul with cowardice
To win tolerance
From the envy that is the hatred
Of raging, rampant, raging mediocrity.
But to win
Brings only sad, lonely pride

And proud, sad loneliness.
And yet I say
That there is no other choice
But death, and double death
Before that final, dying time
Of pain, anguish, agony
Into the surcease
Of nothingness.

And
All men who were,
And all men who are,
And all men who are yet to be,
All are, each and all,
But poor Yorick's brothers.
And victory
Is but these brave deeds
And these proud words
That live alone, beyond
The choking, choked
And silent
Silenced dust
Of all poor Yorick's brothers.

1962

Poem for a children's book

S

is for sun
for kisses
and for soul

For all the such
our hearts
and minds
wish to know
love
wonder

and life for the world

S
is for my
self
your
self
everybody's
self

and for the sun
of the soul
somewhere

1963

Carmelitta Maracci

She seemed to be
All compactness
But she was fire
And beauty.
She was the beauty of fire
As inspiration.
This was when she danced.
Her name was Carmelitta Maracci.
She is said to be Peruvian American.
We who saw her

Remember.
We are still
Remembering.

1963

Friends, Romans, countrymen, and
manipulators!

W e live badly,
Yet it is called good.
We hope in the silence of dreams
That we yet may live.
But the days of our lives
Are traps of Time
Clamping us
Like helpless, wounded animals
Who cannot spring the trap
And bound away in bounding freedom.

So long as we are thus,
So long as we live thus,
Then, to be unhappy
Can be, might be,
And on many a day,
It is better,
Better than to be happy
Through living badly.
What is this,
This living badly,
But a shaming
Of that spirit of man
Which is an aspiration
Grown out of
The cruelty of the long ages.
There is no shame
In unhappiness.

1963

To a girl from Roma

If you were a man,
And I were a woman,
And you wrote a poem
To me,
What would you say
That would not be
The saying
Of what you would want
And hope to gain.
Ti voglio bene.

1963

Waiting

I have been waiting.
I have been waiting
For you.
With nervous hope
I have been waiting
For you to come
To me.
And in my hope
I know you.

1964

Golden youth: 1794

Today, he could be called a lion,
A golden youth.
In David's portrait,
He looks as exquisitely sensitive as a lovely girl.
He wrote when young,
"Happiness is a new idea";
But he was called "L'Ange du Mort."
He wrote when young,
That he could ride the crests of his century,
And that he could stand above misfortune.

He wrote when young
To express the hope
That danger would encompass his "Companions in
    Liberty,"
As he knew that he would be encompassed.
He was young
When he rode in one of the carts
And he heard the noises the tumbrils made,
And the shrieks of the mad Thermadorean mob.
He was young
When he walked up to the guillotine
With proud disdain.
His name was St. Just.
He was one with the Revolution—
Its child.

1963

Fragment on greatness

They want to be great,
As great as their fears
Will permit them to become great.
They know, inside their own selves,
That it is too late,
Too late for greatness.
They are swollen reputations,
Made by the noise
They make,
Plus the noise

That is made for them.
This is just about all
That I have need to say
About them.

1963

Gethsemane

I

How soft can darkness be,
Darkness of the darkest dark night
That man can carry
In his long slow memory
As he travels on
From Life to Death.
There was a night
When the blood of Jesus Christ was sensibility

69

And sensibility was love and poetry
And love and poetry were tragedy
And tragedy was dark, falling
Black blots of blood
From the sweated brow of Jesus Christ
Onto that mass of earth
That was called
Gethsemane.

II

We suffer the sufferings of our own suffering.
We sorrow for our own sorrows.

III

How soft can darkness be.

1964

Love poem

Is there any need
For me
To tell you what you know—
That I love you?
We loved before we met,
We were in love before we met;
We are in love;
We shall be in love for long;
Because we,
Children of defeats and many defeats

Have hopes and dreams.
We loved in our hopes,
And we loved in our dreams
Because we could not live
On yesterday's defeats
And tomorrow's death,
And to live was hope
And it was, also, dreams
Of love, our love.
No, I need not say it,
But I still must say it—
Above death
I love you.

1962

John Fitzgerald Kennedy

He rode, smiling in sun and triumph
Six seconds of naked tragedy
And of the ultimate, terrible beauty of death—
   he was no more.
We wept in the solitudes of our silence,
With the solidarity of grief.

1963

Jackson Park

J ackson Park was green
Forty years ago;
But 1963 was forty years away.
Jackson Park is green again,
With the newest, youngest, greenest green
That we now can know.
But 1923 was forty years ago.

1963

Wearied world

On this always-turning planet,
Earth,
There is change,
And continuity
Of all there is
Upon this always-turning earth;
But there is no death.
But only a chemical change called death
By us and ours,
Who go head up,

And head upside down,
On this always, and still-always-turning
Earth.
In a wearied world,
Change is law,
Beyond our wills—
Always, always, always,
Turning change.

1962

The world is today

The world is today,
And today is today is today
Is always now
And every minute of our lives
Is today, today,
Is always now.
But once upon a time
Was now,
Yesterday was today,
Yesterday was now.

1964

77

Breathless

The Tyranny of Time
Is the Thief of Youth.
This I learned
In the first days of my young manhood.
And this I learned
With anger.
It was an anger of the soul
And it left me
Angry for life.
And angry with life.
It was then

That I began
To run breathless,
Every minute of my life.
And I am running still—
Running.
Breathless.

1962

Index of First Lines

This book has been set in Antique no. 1, and printed on Ivory Stoneridge Paper. The design of text, cover, and jacket is by Betty Binns. The sketch of Mr. Farrell is by Fairfield Porter.

Composed printed and bound by American Book–Stratford Press.